Understanding Nature
By Rick McKeon
Copyright 2014 Rick McKeon

Preface

If you love nature and being outdoors - hiking, smelling the fresh air, and feeling the warm sun on your skin - you will love this book! This little book is filled with activities to increase your enjoyment and understanding of the natural world. Not only will you understand nature at a deeper level, you will start to understand that you are a part of the natural world and it is part of you!

No matter what your experience so far, you can understand nature at a deeper level. And it's not mysterious or hard. In fact it's easy, fun and natural. We have been on this planet a long time and we are meant to be part of the natural world. We are meant to live in harmony with nature!

If you give these activities a try you will be surprised how they will fill you with gratitude and joy.

I would love to hear your comments and suggestions. Send me an email at rmckeon5@gmail.com

Let's get started!
Rick

Table Of Contents

1. Connectedness   5
1.1 How Are the Objects Near You Interconnected?
1.2 You Are Part of Nature!

2. Smell a Tree   8
2.1 Get to Know a Tree

3. Expanding Circles of Awareness   12
3.1 Expanding Circles

4. Be Still and Listen   15
4.1 Be Still and Listen

5. Don't Eat Me!   17
5.1 A Variety of Defense Mechanisms

6. Be in the Moment   20
6.1 How Long?

7. Nature's Geometry   22
7.1 Geometric Patterns in Nature
7.2 Bilateral Symmetry
7.3 Spirals

8. Cycles   27
8.1 Nature's Cycles

9. Just Give Me a Chance   32
9.1 Life Takes Hold!

10. Beauty and the Beast   35
10.1 Look for the Beauty

11. A Multitude of Colors   37
11.1 A Multitude of Colors

12. Seed Dispersal: Can I Hitch a Ride?   38
12.1 Unique Methods - How Many can You Notice?

13. Let's Get Together!   40
13.1 Things That Clump

14. Dragons in the Sky   41
14.1 Patterns

15. Serenity Is Contagious   42
15.1 Can We Communicate Serenity?

16. The Non-Activity   44
16.1 Be Receptive

17. The Filter   45
17.1 Remove the Filter

18. I'm Not Here   47
18.1 Disappear and Observe

19. Conclusion and a Challenge   49
Everything Belongs Here

Contact the Author   50

Other Books By this Author   50

1. Connectedness

"Up here in the mountains it's easy to see how everything is interconnected. Water flows over the rocks and they become smooth like water. The trees are exposed to violent storms and take on a fractured and twisted form like the storms. If you lay down in a lush meadow you can feel the warm sun and the cool, moist grass. Am I connected to and influenced by these lovely surroundings? Yes, I know this for certain!"

I wrote these words while sitting beside Timberline Lake in the Sierra Nevada Mountains of California.

This first activity may be the most important of all the activities in this book. With this activity we introduce the concept that not only can you experience nature at a deeper level - you are *part of* nature and it is part of you! If you can grasp this concept it will change your relationship with this planet forever!

Activity 1.1 How Are the Objects near You Interconnected?

Find a nice comfortable place to sit and relax.

Pick a few objects close to you and see if you can determine how they are connected. How do they influence each other? Here are some ideas to get you thinking:

1. Is there a big rock acting as a heat sink or a windbreak to provide protection for the plants near it?
2. Are the Willow trees here thriving because they are in a wash?
3. Can you see what's happening in the picture above? If you understand this one photograph you are already part of nature! Can you see life and death, the passage of time, nutrients being returned to the soil? Are there processes here that take longer than you will be on this planet?
4. Is the rock you are sitting on smooth? How did it get that way? Is it just part a larger formation (has it broken off from a larger rock)? Can you imagine what it was like several million years ago?
5. Is it cooler here than over there because you are sitting in the shade? Does this constitute an ecosystem?
6. Are the little birds that visit this site just waiting for you to leave so they can get the seeds right in front of you?

Now the important one:

Activity 1.2 You Are Part of Nature!

You are part of your surroundings and your surroundings part of you. At first that concept may seem a little crazy, but try the following:

Take a slow deep breath and imagine the air flowing into you. Picture it. Some of the oxygen in the air gets exchanged in your lungs and becomes part of you (It doesn't just go back out again when you breath out).

When you exhale, the plants near you will absorb some of the carbon dioxide from your body and it will become part of them! In turn, they will return oxygen to you. Picture the exchanges taking place between you and all of nature around you.

In our modern, polluted world we may not want to drink the water from a stream without filtering it. When we are out backpacking we carry water filters just to be safe. Imagine drinking the (filtered) water from a stream. What happens to that water when you drink it? Where does it go?

It becomes part of you. It circulates throughout your body. Eventually you will return it to the earth.

> "One of my fondest memories is of a time when I was floating down a crystal clear river up in the Sierra Nevada Mountains in an inner tube. Everything was perfect and I felt like I was a part of that river. I leaned over and took a sip of the water, and then it hit me. I am a part of this river and it is a part of me! What an exciting moment!"

The same can be said for the plants that we eat. They come from the earth. They become part of us and then we return nutrients to the earth.

You are literally part of nature and nature is part of you. This isn't science fiction or some fantasy - it's just how things work!

With this understanding you can see how important it is that we live in harmony with nature.

2. Smell A Tree

Did you know Ponderosa Pine trees smell like vanilla, White Fir needles smell like oranges and Jeffrey Pine trees smell like butterscotch?

Do you want to experience trees at a deeper, more personal level? This is an activity to help you do exactly that! We are going to use all of our senses and get as close to your favorite tree as we can.

You may hike through the woods and wonder at how beautiful and majestic the trees are. Some are all gnarled and twisted from disease or from a multitude of harsh winters. When this happens to people we don't think it is beautiful, but when it happens to trees we think it adds character. Well, maybe we need to change our thinking!

Enough of that, let's get back to the trees.

Just knowing the name of a tree really doesn't add to our understanding. In fact, it might even limit our understanding. Just knowing the name leads us to think we know something about that tree and we don't need to know any more. Assigning labels can made us complacent in our understanding!

How can we get to know a tree?

Let's look at the Ponderosa Pine, Alligator Juniper and Aspen.

Look at the bark. Notice the color, texture, feel and smell. Could you identify these three even with your eyes closed by their texture or smell?

Obviously the bark of each of these trees is very different. Notice their color and texture. If you touch an aspen tree the white stuff comes off on your hands. The bark of the Ponderosa Pine feels crumbly. Get the idea? We are starting to get to know these trees on a physical level by using the sense of touch.

If you smell them you will notice the Ponderosa Pine smells like vanilla. Do the other trees have a unique smell?

Look at their leaves. Again notice their color, texture and anything else unique about them. How many needles per cluster? How are the leaves situated on the branches? How big are they? Are they stiff or flexible? Is the leafstalk round or flat? Aspen leaves move even with a slight breeze because their leafstalk is flat, not round.

Crumple a leaf and smell it. Probably it has a delightful smell but maybe not. If you dare, taste it with just the tip of your tongue. Mistake? Well, we are getting to know trees at a deeper level.

Activity 2.1 Get to Know a Tree

For this activity we want to get to know a tree in as much detail as possible. We will use all of our senses to understand the tree at a deeper level.

Choose a tree. It doesn't have to be the biggest or even the healthiest one. Just choose one that interests you. How many things are there to learn about this tree? Think about it and then think about it again. See if you can add to the list. I bet if you quiet your mind and think about it the list will grow quite long!

First look at the obvious things and then more subtle things. Here is a partial list of things to learn about this tree.

1. It's size and overall shape.
2. Is this tree young or older? How will it change as it gets older?
3. It's branches – do they go up and out, droop down?
4. The leaves – broad leaves or needles? If needles, how many per group? Color, thickness, shape, smell, feel (smooth and soft, hard and brittle, sharp points, etc.)
5. It's bark – color, thickness, texture, smell, taste, and spikes?
6. Close up – What are the smallest details you can notice? Do you need to come back with a magnifying glass to see details in the bark or veins in the leaves?

7. Touch this tree. Does it bring back any memories – maybe from your childhood, maybe from your honeymoon!
8. Is this tree used commercially? What properties does it have that make it suitable for commercial use?

Why does it have these features?

1. Desert plants need to preserve moisture so they have a waxy coating or small surface area on the leaves. If the leaves are small, maybe the bark itself is green and photosynthetic.
2. Thick fire-resistant bark?
3. Hard or sharp parts provide protection.
4. Deep taproots or shallow roots near the surface to capture even the lightest rain.

3. Expanding Circles of Awareness

Find a beautiful place to sit and relax for a while. Forget about all of your problems and just be here in this one place. Start to notice the amazing things all around you.

In this activity you are going to become aware of your surroundings. It starts from deep within your own body and expands in ever widening circles until you are aware of all things.

I'm asking you to apply all of your five senses and maybe even more. How about your sense of the past? The history of this place? You might think, "How can I know the history of this place just by looking?" If you understand a little bit of geology you can imagine what it was like here a million years ago! If you observe the trees and plants around you right now, you might get a glimpse of how things were last winter or maybe a hundred years ago. How about the emotions that are flowing into you right now because of the sun and smell of the grass you're sitting on? Where do they come from? What is the texture of the rocks, trees and soil near you? Think about the time of year and the season of your own life right now. We're talking about close observation of your surroundings combined with introspection.

It might be easy to notice things close to us, but we can also notice things that are far away. Let me tell you a story about what happened to me when I was taking a nap in my dorm room at college.

> "I was taking a nap, just lying on my bed resting when I heard this strange sound. It was like, "ching, ching, ching, ching . . ." and I wondered, "What is that sound?" Well, it turns out it was my wristwatch. I had my hands clasped behind my head and my (mechanical) wristwatch was close to my left ear. That was pretty interesting, so I gradually moved my hand out and started listening for that sound. When I had my arm fully extended I could still hear it! So I started moving the watch further and further away, and when I had it setting on the dresser across the room I could still hear the ticking of that watch! I was tuned in to that sound and could still hear it! This was amazing and I wondered what else I could hear? That was my introduction to the whole concept of sensitivity."

In our modern, fast-paced world we bump along just trying to keep up. Many times we are completely unaware of our surroundings. Can we get back to the place our ancestors were when they depended on their senses for survival? Can we get in touch with the natural world all around us? This activity is not hard or painful. It's easy and natural. This is an activity designed to help you become more aware of your natural surroundings.

Activity 3.1 Expanding Circles of Awareness

This activity can be conducted anywhere, but it's best if you are in a pleasant natural environment. Get away from the noise and confusion of the city and find a quiet place.

First start with yourself. Concentrate on your own breathing. Listen for your own heartbeat. Become completely relaxed and at peace with yourself and the world around you. Here's where it starts.

Now we are going to expand the circle of awareness. If you are in a lovely place this is going to be a lot of fun!

Notice what's just around you in a ten-foot circle. Notice as much as you can. Take in all the detail. Here's where we use all of our senses to become immersed in our surroundings - colors, textures, the soft grass, the damp mud, the sharp spines on hard leaves, crumbly or smooth bark on trees, rocks that have been waiting millions of years for you to notice them.

Are there an amazing variety of colors within the ten-foot circle from where you sit? What can you hear? Can you hear the wind, the stream next to you, insects or birds? There is a lot going on in this ten-foot circle! Has ten feet ever contained so much?

Let all that settle in for a while and then expand your circle to 20 feet. Are there things here you didn't notice in the ten-foot circle? Don't worry if you wear glasses or not. Maybe the detail is not as important now. Does the wind bring things into this circle from far away? Are there trees here that you didn't notice in the ten-foot circle or maybe have never noticed before? Do the gullies start to open up? Does the landscape start to make more sense? Are you part of a bigger community?

Let's expand the circle to 50 feet. Now all things are possible! How many things are actually here that weren't in your smaller circles? Think about all the philosophical implications. Can we grow bigger if we start by understanding what is close to us and then expand our view? If you can hear a wristwatch close to your ear, can you hear it across the room? Can you hear people or animals or plants in need? Can we touch the natural world that is close to us? Can we be touched by those that are far away?

4. Be Still and Listen

This activity is both restful and exciting. Like the "Expanding Circles of Awareness" this exercise will open up your senses – and hopefully your soul – to the world around you. For this activity we are going to focus on the sense of hearing. When we are going about our daily business we miss out on fully ninety percent of what our environment holds! We are preoccupied with the task at hand and we block out everything else.

What kinds of sounds does nature produce? I bet you will be amazed at what you will hear! So, here's the activity:

Activity 4.1 Be Still and Listen

Find a comfortable spot to stand or sit. Now we're going to start to connect with our surroundings by listening. At first you will hear the obvious stuff, but then you will start to become aware of more subtle sounds. You may hear the wind. Is it far away or close? Can you tell which direction it is moving? If it's moving toward you, track it's motion until it reaches your location and then continue to track it as it moves off.

You may hear water flowing. Can you detect different sounds as the water splashes or flows over a small falls? Are there recurring sounds? If so, are they periodic?

You may hear trees rubbing against each other or the sound of cars from a distant highway or jet airplanes flying overhead. Are there birds here? Do they seem to be talking to each other? What are they saying – a mating call, a warning? Can you hear a squirrel scampering around?

It's fall now and the leaves are falling. The other day I was on a hike and the wind caused a shower of leaves. I could actually hear the leaves hit the ground! As you quiet your mind and body you will hear amazing things, and when you leave this place you will know it better.

After note: You can do this activity anywhere, even at home in your living room. Just take some time to be still and listen.

5. Don't Eat Me!

I went out one morning and found this pretty little spotted moth on my front porch. When I touched him he popped open his wings to reveal a bright orange color with black spots. Frankly I was startled and started thinking this must be a defense mechanism to scare off predators.

All animals and plants have some kind of defense mechanism.

I was out on a hike just yesterday and, out of the corner of my eye, noticed some movement. I turned just in time to see a deer bound off into the woods. A deer is not going to stand and fight. No, his defense is agility and speed. The same thing can be said for the little lizards I see every day. They are predators but when they see a big thing like me they take off fast!

Think about the following:

1. Cacti have sharp spines.
2. Walking Sticks look like sticks!
3. Some butterflies have spots that look like big eyes.
4. Many insects fly an irregular path. I always used to wonder, "How come they fly all over the place instead of just going straight to their destination?" Who's smarter - me or the butterfly?
5. If you touch a "tip-up bug" he will tip up and just hold still. Maybe he thinks he looks like a rock.
6. A glass snake will actually drop off a piece of his tail.
7. Ever smell a skunk?

Here are some photos to get you thinking about defense mechanisms in plants and animals. In the first one you will have to look close to see the walking stick, but he's there!

Activity 5.1 A Variety of Defense Mechanisms

As you are hiking along start to notice the plants, animals and insects all around you. If they didn't have defense mechanisms and didn't know how to survive they would have gone extinct long ago. Keep a tally and see how many different ingenious defense mechanisms you can find.

6. Be in the Moment

"This is what I came here for. All the sweat and struggle to get here is distilled in this one precious drop of time! Here is the confluence of all that is beauty and wonder! The flow of bright sun combines with that of sparkling water and soothing breezes to create that special magic moment we only experience once in a great while!

I don't understand it. All things combine to create this moment and I want to hang on to it as long as I can. No wonder I am drawn back to the Sierra again and again."

I recorded those words while taking a rest break along the John Muir Trail. I was completely in the moment – not thinking about the past or the future.

Activity 6.1 How Long?

In our busy, hectic lives we are used to going "a mile a minute" and thinking about ten things at once. We take multitasking to an extreme so that we are even rude and don't give others our full attention when talking to them. Have you ever been on the phone and were tempted to type on the computer keyboard? The other person can hear your keystrokes!

Let's get out in nature where there are no distractions, quiet our minds, and see how long we can be in the moment. This exercise may be difficult at first, but I bet you will get better with practice and you will enjoy it more and more.

Find a nice quiet place to relax. Take a few deep breaths and each time you exhale see your stresses flowing out of your body. Now pick an object somewhere near you and see how long you can think about just that one object without other things crowding into your mind.

How long was it - two seconds, ten seconds, a minute? Well, give it another try. Put everything else out of your mind and concentrate on that stream or tree or whatever it is you have chosen.

How did you do? Were you able to concentrate a little bit longer? If you did, that's great! Don't make work out of it but try this activity every now and then and see if it doesn't have a calming effect.

7. Nature's Geometry

When you are out in nature you will notice an amazing variety of geometric patterns. Plants, animals and insects together with rocks, wind and water interact to create a symphony of geometric shapes! Here are a few pictures to get you thinking about the geometry of nature.

Activity 7.1 Geometric Patterns in Nature

Look for geometric shapes in the natural world around you. If you look closely you will see triangles, squares and pentagons. You will also see circles and spirals. For this activity take note of how many different geometric patterns you can see. Some of them might be mixed or imperfect. Some of them might be "almost but not quite" perfect shapes. If so, why? Does it have to do with weather conditions, fire or insects?

Bilateral Symmetry

That may seem like a pretty technical term, but it just means something that is similar on either side of the center. Think of the human face – you have two eyes, two ears and two nostrils pretty evenly spaced on either side of the center (hopefully). Also you have two arms, two legs, etc. on opposite sides of the body.

Many things in nature exhibit bilateral symmetry and many don't. Here are a few examples of bilateral symmetry in nature.

Activity 7.2 Bilateral Symmetry

Pick a small area to explore and see how many examples of bilateral symmetry you can find. Keep in mind its not just plants we are looking for. Most animals, insects, and many crystals exhibit this property.

Spirals In Nature

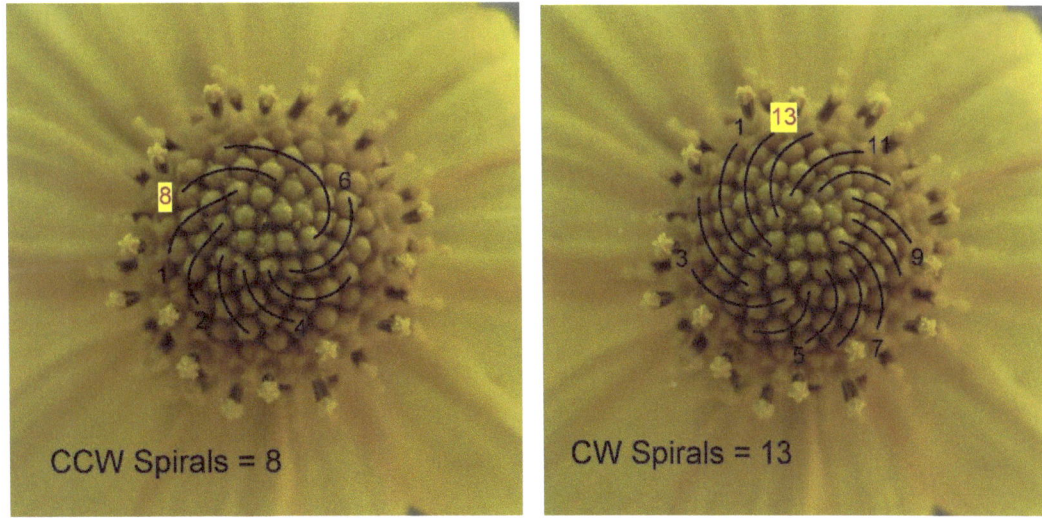

CCW Spirals = 8

CW Spirals = 13

Most flowers, pinecones, and acorns have spiral patterns that go both clockwise and counterclockwise. The amazing thing is that, if you count them, the number of spirals usually seems to be consecutive Fibonacci numbers!

What are Fibonacci numbers you ask? It's a pretty simple but amazing sequence. Fibonacci numbers are generated by simply adding the previous two numbers to get the next one. So, the Fibonacci sequence is:

1, 1, 2, 3, 5, 8, 13, 21, 34, 55, . . .

See how it works?

Activity 7.3 Spirals

Find a pinecone or a flower and notice the spiral patterns. See if you can count the number clockwise and counterclockwise spirals. Do they turn out to be consecutive Fibonacci numbers?

In the field it may help to put a little mark at your starting point with a magic marker to keep from getting lost as you work your way around.

An even easier method is to take a picture and print it out at home. Then you can mark it up with a pencil or colored magic marker.

Of course the question is, "Why?" Why do they tend to be Fibonacci Spirals? The sequence is built on growth, as are the natural objects you are observing. What's the connection?

8. Cycles

Nature's cycles are endless, amazing and interconnected. Look at the photograph above. It's easy to see the old, dead tree and the young seedling. But what else do you see? Can you see the mycelium? What role does it play in this cycle? Are there other helper plants or animals enriching the soil here?

All things exhibit cycles - animals, plants and even the earth itself. The cycles of nature may be long or short. From sub-atomic particles to the universe itself these cycles may take microseconds or billions of years! Think about life and death and then new life. Think about day and night, the earth revolving around the sun, or the life cycles of stars.

Getting to know nature at a deeper level involves understanding cycles and where we are in those cycles. The following pictures depict the life cycle of a tree from seedling to mature tree and then a fallen tree returning it's nutrients back to the soil to nurture yet another seedling.

Activity 8.1 Nature's Cycles

For some this might be sobering, but nature's cycles should be inspiring to us! After all, we are part of many different cycles happening all at once. Shakespeare said, "We strut and fret our hour upon the stage and then are no more." As we understand nature in a deeper way we can see many more cycles than simply our life on this planet. So here's the activity:

Find a beautiful place to conduct this activity. It might be a quiet stream in a lush valley or it might be a barren spot out in the desert. You can observe nature's cycles anywhere. Now, have a look around. We're looking for cycles of life or activity, short or long. We want to understand these cycles and where we are in them.

You may see insects, animals, or rock and water interacting. What is happening here? How long does this cycle take? Is it fall and the leaves are dropping? Is it spring and little shoots are just coming up? Look for movement and interaction. Can you become a greater part of what you see around you? This is you becoming part of nature.

9. Just Give Me a Chance!

This planet is teeming with life!

Thankfully, life can take hold in the most unlikely places. We see life flourishing in hot springs, dry deserts and cold mountaintops. Given even the slightest chance life will take hold.

What's happening in the picture above? There is a little crack in the rock. In that crack there must have been some dirt blown in or maybe washed down from above. Then a seed was deposited - maybe by the wind; maybe it passed through a bird's system unharmed. So, it was able to germinate and take hold. You may think its odds of survival are slim but look at the next few photographs.

Even after a devastating fire the flowers return!

Activity 9.1 Life Takes Hold!

In this activity we are going to look for (and hopefully be amazed by) the tenacity of life, and come to appreciate how our lovely planet is the perfect place for life to flourish.

This activity will work anywhere so I don't need to set the stage. Wherever you are, just stop and look around. We're looking for life, but most especially we're looking to see life flourishing in the most unlikely places. It could be in the forest or in a crack in the road. Look closely and see how life succeeds. I would love to hear about your discoveries, so send me an email.

10. Beauty and the Beast

So many times in nature we see a tree that is gnarled and twisted, and we think it has beauty and character. But if a person is gnarled and twisted we don't think it is beautiful. We don't think about the storms and trials that have created character in that person. Does he have wisdom gained through life's trials that he can impart to me? Does he have something special to teach?

The burl in the photograph below could be sold for hundreds of dollars. We would consider it a prize and turn it into beautiful wooden panels or tabletops.

Activity 10.1 Look for the Beauty

Stop along your favorite hiking trail and look for unusual things. Are there things here that we find interesting, unusual or beautiful? If we saw these same things in a person would we appreciate them less or consider them repulsive? Are we so different from the natural world all around us?

Can you apply this lesson to the people in your life? Maybe someone has a difficult personality, a physical ailment or is different in some way. Can you see the beauty and special character in them?

11. A Multitude of Colors

Everywhere you look nature displays a multitude of colors! Animals, plants, insects, and even in lichen you will find an amazing array of colors.

Activity 11.1 A Multitude of Colors

On your next outing pick a place at random and look to see how many different colors and shades of color you can find. Don't be in a hurry. Once you think you have found them all – look again. I bet you will be amazed!

12. Seed Dispersal: Can I Hitch a Ride?

Plants have developed an amazing variety of methods to disperse their seeds. How many can you think of? Here are a few photographs to get you thinking.

Activity 12.1 Unique Methods - How Many Can You Notice?

This activity works best in the fall of the year when plants have gone to seed. Just stop and look closely at the plants that have produced seeds. They want to disperse their seeds as widely as possible for survival of the species. See how many different methods you can observe. Will they be dispersed by hitching a ride on passing animals, being caught up in the wind, or by being eaten and deposited later in a different place?

13. Let's Get Together!

If you spend much time outdoors you will notice that many times things seem to gather together in organized colonies or just clump up, forming patterns. In the picture above small twigs have been washed down a hiking trail. They aren't just spread out over the trail in random fashion. For some reason, they have started to clump up and form a pattern. In fact, the pattern seems pretty regular like a washboard on a dirt road.

As part of our study of nature we want to understand why things happen the way they do.

Activity 13.1 Things That Clump Together

Look around and notice how patterns seem to emerge from randomness. Even inanimate objects like fallen twigs or rocks seem to desire order and structure. Can you notice some patterns starting to emerge in places where things should be just random and evenly distributed? There are some natural forces at work here!

14. Dragons in the Sky

When we were kids we would lie on our backs in the grass and look up at the clouds. We could imagine all kinds of animals and faces in the clouds – dragons, ships and monsters! To really appreciate nature it's important to retain some of that childlike wonder.

Activity 14.1 Patterns

Take some time to be a kid again. Just enjoy finding patterns in the clouds. We can still get lost in this exciting activity as adults. The human mind has the ability to "connect the dots" and see patterns that may or may not exist. If the patterns are real (as in the picture above) what causes them? Do you know the different types of clouds (cirrus, nimbus, stratus . . .) and how they are formed? It would be a fun quest to see how many different types of clouds you can identify in your area. As you can see, this could turn out to be a huge study, but for this exercise just enjoy the beauty and variety of clouds.

15. Serenity Is Contagious

"I was out hiking in the desert one evening just around sunset. It was a beautiful, calm evening and I felt at peace with everything around me. It was one of those special magic moments! Then I noticed a young coyote coming up towards me. Normally I would have thought, 'Will it bite me? Does it have rabies?' But I was at peace that evening, and just stood still as he approached. He came within a few feet of me, and we just stood there exchanging glances. Evidently he could sense that there was no danger. After a while he turned and walked off. I was amazed!"

Activity 15.1 Can We Communicate Serenity?

We have talked earlier about natural defense mechanisms. All animals and plants have evolved defense mechanisms for survival and that is a good thing. But, if you are not a threat can they sense it? You know you are starting to integrate yourself into nature if the animals and plants around you are willing to give up their natural defense mechanisms in order to come in contact with you.

So, here's the activity. Sit quietly and imagine yourself as part of everything around you. You are just like the little brook that flows beside you. You are just like the trees surrounding you or the rock your sitting on. If you see a butterfly, silently call him to you. Hold out your hand for him to land on. Be patient, not demanding. Butterflies fly an irregular path as a natural defense, but if you are not a threat he will come to you. If you hear birds, try to mimic their call and see if they will talk to you or come over for a visit.

If the animals can see that you are not a threat and are attracted to you, this is a good sign you are becoming one with nature.

16. The Non-Activity

This activity may seem a little strange at first, but give it a try.

Instead of following a plan or trying to focus on some aspect of your surroundings, just sit quietly and be receptive. This time we are not in charge. We are not directing the show. Think of it as going to a theater to see a show you have never seen before.

Activity 16.1 Be Receptive

The way to receive new thoughts and insights is to just sit and listen without any expectations and see what thoughts come. Just be still, listen and wait. Who knows what will happen? You may receive a flash of inspiration. Maybe nothing will happen. If nothing happens that doesn't mean you shouldn't try this activity again in the future.

17. The Filter

Everything we perceive (see, hear, smell, taste, feel) is filtered somehow before it reaches our brain. None of our senses are perfect. In fact, many species have senses that are keener than ours in some ways!

But the filter that clouds our perception the most and separates us from nature is the busy and chaotic state of our thoughts. It's so easy to be preoccupied with concerns and worries about everyday living. These thoughts block our perception of the natural world all around us.

Activity 17.1 Remove the Filter

Picture your worries and preoccupations as mental filters like funny colored sunglasses that obscure your vision. In this activity we are going to take those glasses off and see clearly.

Relax your mind. Forget your cares and concerns about work, family or finances. Just put them aside for a while. Take off those filters and look around with clear vision. You are now free to see more clearly and in greater detail. What do you see?

18. I'm Not Here

So many times when we are out in nature our very presence is a disruptive force. Can you make yourself "invisible" so that the animals go about their lives as if you were not there? Hunters try to do this with tree blinds, camouflage and scent free clothing. Our purpose isn't to disappear so we can shoot them, but so we can observe them more closely.

Activity 18.1 Disappear and Observe

When you first arrive you will probably be a loud, disruptive force and all the animals will be aware of your presence. But if you give it some time, sit quietly and "disappear" things will settle down and you will be able to observe nature is it is. How can you do this?

Find a comfortable spot to sit so you won't have to squirm around and make noise. Just sit quietly and be an observer.

19. Conclusion and a Challenge

We've done several activities to help us understand nature at a deeper level. Hopefully you have enjoyed these activities and have a greater appreciation for and understanding of your place in the natural world. So, in conclusion, let me get a little bit "preachy." I call this, "Everything Belongs Here."

Look at everything in your surroundings and notice how each thing belongs there. Notice how it has adapted to its specific ecosystem and the entire world. Spend some time, and see the relationships between things.

Nature is not something for us to use and just use up! We need to learn to live in harmony with the natural world.

Think about our "nest" our planet - the atmosphere, the soil, flowing streams, and the little bird that lands on your back porch. Think about monoculture, pesticides, pollution and soil depletion. Think about the inhumane way we raise animals for slaughter and the way we treat this planet.

We belong on this planet. We have a place here, but we can ruin it for ourselves. We won't destroy the planet. The earth is going to be around for a long time. BUT we might just make it uninhabitable for humans. What happens when the human species has gone extinct? Well, then others will have their chance to flourish and become the dominant species.

Maybe the ants.

Contact The Author

Your comments are always welcome. Send me an email at rmckeon5@gmail.com

Other Books by this Author

See my website for details https://www.rickmckeonNature.com

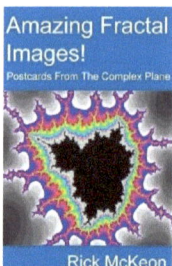 Amazing Fractal Images: Postcards From the Complex Plane
ISBN: 9781311990440

 Sierra Impressions: Images and Inspiration From the Sierras
ISBN: 9781310403699

 Underlying Patterns: The Search for Patterns in Nature
ISBN: 9781311783615

 You Make Us Feel Young Again!
ISBN: 9781310558108